TODAY'S SPECIAL DISH

Today's Special Dish NINA LINDSAY

POEMS

SIXTEEN RIVERS PRESS

"The Round." Copyright © 1985 by Stanley Kunitz,
from *Passing Through: The Later Poems New and Selected*
by Stanley Kunitz. Used by permission of W.W. Norton & Company, Inc.

Grateful acknowledgment is made to the following journals, in which
many of these poems first appeared, sometimes in different form: *88*,
Gastronomica (University of California Press), *Green Mountains Review*,
In the Grove, *Many Mountains Moving*, *POOL*, *Porcupine*, *RATTLE*, *Sow's
Ear Poetry Review*, and *Spillway*.

My gratitude goes to the Sunday-night writers' group, the equinox and
solstice writing group, Sixteen Rivers Press, and to the friends, family,
and teachers who have encouraged and supported me. Special thanks
also goes to the people who make my workday enjoyable: those who
make and serve my coffee and my lunch so graciously, the bus drivers
and the BART conductors, the gardeners at the Oakland Museum and
the tenders of its turtle pond, the coworkers who ask me how it's going,
and the many strangers I've passed on the street who have smiled and
said "Good afternoon."

Cover photo: "Ozzie's" by Nina Lindsay
Author photo: Benjamin Tice Smith
Cover and interior design: David Bullen

ISBN 13: 978-0-9767642-3-6
LCN: 2006909778

Printed in Canada

for Max

POEMS

It's Wednesday

It's Wednesday,

and the morning sky convulses with the sounds
of garbage, almost as lovely

as the ocean, almost as regular.
My waking body opens from the middle; tight-

fisted dreams start to break apart like lightly tethered snores: "ask
Lisa if she ordered paper for the copier"—the note

I didn't write, yesterday at closing, now baffles
round the unhemmed edges of my sleep.

My semiliterate angels wake me,
the garbage truck grinds out its good-bye like the off-

key twangs of a Goodwill guitar,
the day feels old already as I unroll it, smooth it,

smooth it till it's wrinkle free enough to wear again.

Toward a theory of invisibility

It has to do with the density of the body,
the attraction of its atoms.

I practice while I'm bicycling to work,
take stock of my contents: sleepiness,

a heartbeat scaling up the hour
assisted by caffeine,

two books, a bike lock, wallet,
lotion, usual assortment

of miscellany, a memory
of uneasiness, regret

masquerading as gruffness,
a list of things to do as soon

as I walk through the library door,
a slight desire

to veer from the path,
a full bladder, a leather-

bound notebook, and a pen.
The whole of me thus analyzed

into its familial and bickering parts,
I simply portion

my precious allotment of contentment
equitably between them, whisper

go.
And as I turn

the first crank down the hill and pick up speed,
I feel the sizzle as my molecules depart,

happy by themselves,
leaving me

with myself
without myself

at least until it's time to show up at work—
and I tug lightly at my sleeves.

Thursday, I think

After Chinese food last night,
I dreamed of croissants—all
through the tangible

rainy hours before waking.
Now the storm passes,
morning arrives,

suddenly it's light (well,
sort of a half-hearted attempt), and
here I am, armed with coffee, still whole

and getting ready
for what another day will do to me.
There'll be that bundled rush to the station,

the exit gates at my arrival, people
so polite the line never moves.
My library,

hot and creaking, the nervous rustle
of administrators passing
on their way upstairs. A lunch hour

full and gleaming,
and then the afternoon delivered
like some treat I'd craved and dreamed of and forgotten,

in which the eight-year-old
who kicked me when he was seven
will check out *Pippi Longstocking*

with happiness
and impunity
and will pass through the security gates, casual and fearless.

Friday, but I may not make it

The morning starts to rattle.
Helicopters raptor the accident.
I am waiting
for a bus that is surely not coming,

as surely as I must make
my 9:30 meeting. I sit down
on "Fuck you Shelley Foster,"
watch the strawberry-whipped-cream cakes

in the bakery window glimmer
like overdone metaphors
of blissful encounters.
The morning glimmers back,

convincing as the green light's chirp.
The garbage truck keeps grinding.
Beauty keeps failing. Even
so, I look down the street. Sun

glints off windshields,
seeds of hope, good
intentions, all sorts of things
that almost look like buses, from a distance.

Don't run yet,

no need to raise
the pair of huddled pigeons from their wire, articulate

feather
feathering feather, no sense to startle

the morning caféers, settled into their con-
versations like little

spoons against the lips of saucers—
one woman

staring at mid-distance, light
across her face and liking

herself—
no need to rumble

the dream that's settled in my feet like
syrup in the bottom of the bottle;

though the train is considering the tunnel,
though the minute shoulders closer,

don't run yet, though I'll have to,
run for it,

soon.

It does

I can scarcely wait till tomorrow
when a new life begins for me,
as it does each day,
as it does each day.
from "The Round," by Stanley Kunitz

I'd like to think about this one for a bit.
The job, though appealing

in certain moments and from a distance,
mostly involves people who don't like each other

in a building all day together. Adults
despise each other so freely, yet never

it seems, while eating lunch. I'm returning from it
when the silhouette of someone with your gait,

though too tall to be you, returns my heart.
Street trees flat-topped just below the wires

are sending out new arms. I can only think
that morning must be nostalgic for itself —why else

would it keep coming back, allowing us
to blow things on a daily basis?

At the corner, the planks of a demolished house crawl up
each other in a pile, remembering floors and walls.

I get back to work. The same people
are all fed and pleasant. Afternoon

sweeps in with its apologies, too familiar,
once again, to be refused.

About the pile on my office desk

Papers nest, caught up
in their tasks, moving
gently, like a lightly caffeinated body,

from one end of the blotter to the other.
The little Post-It notes
no longer sticky, bearing

one word or three in my frantic hand, gone
soft at the corners, barely cling
to the sheer surfaces of the memos, the photo-

copied petty cash receipts
waiting to be filed. They've layered themselves
like a brain: one

that knows what needs to be done.
Mine is the one to do it, but right now it is busy
enjoying the start of one more cup,

watching the far-off surface of the morning begin to shimmer
in the heat, wondering what it is really
that this day needs to be filled with,

and how well accomplished is the thing done
that no one enjoyed doing.

Meanwhile, the pile I have stopped writing about
keeps on being a pile; it shifts
and holds, ripening

like some huge
thorned and enigmatic fruit—the kind
you have to let sit until it really starts to stink

before you sit down at the table and get your fingers to the luscious meat.

Seat available

Because I am alone, I slide onto the stool,
wool on vinyl, just to feel my arms

join the row of arms against the counter.
Knees. Hips. Coats dangle

and kiss. We each study our reading material:
the book, the paper, the menu,

the clock, the waitress, the window.
The paper again—it may have changed.

On the street, people rush at angles with the dust and sirens.
A bus pulls up and everyone tries to get

right where they think it's going to stop. They lunge for the open doors,
and moments later, they're all on—I can see them

through their window, through my window—relax
into the space around each other's shoulders as the bus

pulls out to the light. At the empty stop, the air
heaves its wings, folds them back.

Adults are funny creatures.
Here on my right, one sucks at his coffee, arranges

his fork. "Gotta do the right thing, that's all,"
he says, to everyone in particular,

"Jesus ain't comin' back."
We consider. Clarity absent,

as expected. Still, we wait for it.
Such a good seat, we feel lucky.

Nothing like

the vague squeeze of afternoon to let us hope
the present moment
is the most important. The future

possibly dry, possibly
light and glorious. Yesterday
a slanted proof,

quaint and full
of worn purses and poor avenues
that chase through the grass, fade to night.

Somehow
our lives became more important
than ourselves, developed

national marketing campaigns.
We wait eagerly
for the early reviews.

And while the famous author was addressing the hotel pool

in preview of her public talk, smoothing her words out
along the kind audience of ripples

the bank manager was hauling his dry cleaning in a granny cart and whistling
"Mein Herr" from *Cabaret* a little flat

and the BART police dog was waiting on the platform, waiting for the flicker,
paws aching to scatter across the concrete and up to the beautiful hand

and the librarian was packing up her lunch in just
the way she wished her mother would have done when she was seven

and the house painter was writing poetry in the back seat
of his cousin's hand-me-down Mercedes

and the mayor was reviewing his shoes

and the chickens were beginning to squawk

and the rhododendrons were opening toward their doom

and the author pocketed her notes

and the sun rose in riotous applause above the hotel roof.

Working Saturdays

It seems that things might be all right.
One-handed on the train, I hold the perfect book. People

on the escalator stand
right, walk left, and a week

like a train wreck has
resolved itself as art.

The book ends, and it turns out
I am not the only one with the idea

that hope moves and shifts. Here it is,
my desk. The email opens, and little blue numbers

sort down through the folders. An early arrival
clamors at the locked door

of the library. Behind her
a Pop-Tart-frenzied boy is trying to grab

a balloon without a string,
and the filthy sparrows

bathe in the puddles, mad with industry
and an odd strain of delight.

Morning, noon, and night

The sun came, and then the fog.
The duck stopped quacking like a car alarm.
There was little traffic on the road, not bad; there was
a child who shouted with joy getting into the car
at eight A.M.

There were street trees braving their cages,
there were newspapers without owners,
and the mustardy smells of lunch.
There was a woman afraid of what she was about to do.
There was a clicking of heels.

There was the compass declining.
Birds loving their black shadows.
A trembling in the leaves. A horizon
like the end of the page. There was one hand
held by another, palm to palm, turning back and forth.

HERO PORTRAITS   *audio tour also available*

Self-Portrait in a Box

Let's see if I can remember.
I said "Hold it."
They were going to arrest me, but I

refused to be arrested.
Right hand, you've done good.
Left hand, you've done good.

Self-Portrait in a Toaster

Let me tell you,
we had to dance with each other,
there was no one else around.

The kettle wheezed a tango;
the kitchen light demanded it.

Untitled (verso of *Untitled*)

Let's wait. It's hard
to hold up the corners like this.
My feathers, my feathers.

This is not what was promised.
But look at it—the high and
billowing noises,

the vines and yeasty
smells. Children throwing oranges
into the river. My window,
so uncomfortable, so precious.

The Approximate Man

Let's not go there—
the sublime aspect, the cheerful aspect.
Just wait till they find out.

I really didn't want to have to do this.

Sort of an Indestructible Man

Let me show you my family of cameras.
They watch out for me,
even from here,

so I don't have to worry, it's all
being recorded—my careless
lumbering, the dangerous

directions, the persistent
worrying—they see it all and report
in the evening: dark

and light, dark and light.

Man with a Wing

Let's do that trick your mother hates.
Trying to hold a horse in my arms.
Arranging the flowers with diligence and risk.

Untitled (formerly *Self-Portrait*)

Let's not waste any more time.
I love bargains. There's one stall here
with nothing but radios. People

love radios. Strange,
I can't remember myself
ever listening to one. But you

I can still picture, half-
listening to some comedy, eating noodles,
and newspapers strewn

across the floor. The mountains
outside the crooked window,
and the saint of inner light

adjusting the frame with both hands.

I'LL BE BACK IN AN HOUR OR SO

I'll be back in an hour or so

Pear trees bloom as quietly
as the silky underbelly of a cloudy day. Light

begins to build behind a certain swell.
Hills huddle close as flannel.

Now the day starts
to turn around this point, twisting

like a spine that needs a crack.
In an instant, all history up to this moment

and especially this morning—all its un-
remitting small annoyances—will be wrung out, extinguished,

and there'll be just me,
and everyone else,

and the pear blossoms,
and many sighs of relief.

Aspiration

I want to be a better person
than other people.
Not need to compare myself all the time to them.

Better to be like the dollar bill so good it purrs into the slot,
like the socks you always pick first from the drawer,
like the duck who waddles down the road, observant, concerned,

but relaxed—bizarre and beautiful. The morning wraps its arms around her
and when it is too much she shrugs it back a step
with a bristle of her wings.

Resist

Fog covers noon like neglect,
high and full of shadowless

light that shows nothing;
drifts, backlit, in the sky's shallows like

a beautiful headache, intricate
and shielding,

like the humors that sift
and swirl through the body, beautiful

still body, steady, going
nowhere, unlistening, moving

but barely.

Resent

I never wanted this much feeling
inhabiting me, never wanted to be this

small and calcifying creature, skin gone to horn,
quiet and unreceiving.

In the dream, I am in-
side out and hollow, smooth

and forgiving—like a long-
cherished boat whose hull is being

stroked and admired, free of barnacles,
raised for its cleaning.

Restore

As if it could be put back whole,
the garden choked

with morning glories. As if what occurs
runs circularly, and not

past us, just
too far to grab hold.

I don't want to like
the people I don't like

anymore, but when I did
it was so easy—

There is nothing of the shape of it to salvage
and the ground below is full of shoots

tunneling up,
glorious and indiscriminate.

All I can say is,

Thank God, summer, ripe
with fallacies, has fallen over. Now late November

shakes and rattles
like a shopper thoughtlessly racing his cart
down the splendid aisles. My work

builds itself up like a dog's winter coat, like layers
of blankets, like the way

the crime rate increases, one
person's one unforgivable bad decision
after another, until

we're all double-checking locks with chilly fingers. Until I,
still beating back the night with a second cup of coffee,

look out at the fog and drizzle, the rain
puddles, little mashes of color, the
persimmon tree ablaze with squirrel-

bitten fruit, the shreds
of Tyvek curling from our uncompleted house,

the bottle collector to whom I have not offered
a pair of gloves,
and the pulpy leaf-clogged gutters,

and the soft pits in my heart,
and my thousand particular failures,

and I sit here cracking nuts,
so hard and sweet, and only
this good at this, my favorite time of year.

Motion study

HORTICULTURE: from Latin *hortus* (enclosure),
and *colere* (to revolve, move around, sojourn, dwell).
American Heritage Dictionary of Indo-European Roots

The calla lily curves its belly
against the twisted trunk of oak,
as if it had read some book
on how best to go about this—

the chapter on espalier,[1] its shapes: *cordon,*
palmette, the multiple u-form—
perhaps it peeked through
our bedroom window, saw

how our ankles grow together, bodies
arched and splayed in sleep against the bedding.
Fan shape with oblique branches.
Belgian fence. Diagonal lattice.

1. (Espalier, or "trellis":
training a tree flat, and shaped,
along some surface. Its form (*form,*
from Greek *morph* ("change"), possibly

via Etruscan), that finc line between
what is created (Latin, "grow") and hand-
worked. Constructed. As all
our best things are.)

The lily stakes its space in wind and scent
and air, nearly infinitely flexible, yet: only there,
and there, is where it bends. As we make
ourselves by moving, even

in the effort to stay still.
Root, wend, dwell,
inhabit—reaching for some sun,
or whatever else we call it.

Overture

Allegro ma non troppo

My neighbors each appear with mud shoes, clippers,
behind the rampant radish blooms, bent double,
summoned by the frayed remains of storm clouds
dissipating in the weekend morning's winter light.

I pull out old roots. Earthworms, sow bugs,
ice-aged nameless things with pincers tremble
as I topple stalks of last year's Brussels sprouts.
The dirt beneath is dark, as if there never was such a thing as color.

    Alice prunes her roses. Jonah sifts the compost
    in his purple training underpants. My husband lifts
    the cover of his beehive, where dark and minute
    impulses blink on and off like breath—

And Adriana works on her espalier, planning
its progression like an uncoiling calculus equation in her head.
Her Felcos snip each stray shoot to the nub.
Bedsheets snap up on the line. The breeze is almost warm.

Adagio

Our method for today:
to turn each branch, and patch of dirt,

each unclothed neck
and leg and arm to its logical extension:

touched by light at every angle.
Small birds rummage in the lint and bramble.

At the cleared head of the path, I need a second
cup of tea before I haul the piles away.

My husband notices the invading ants
along the hive. In a moment,

he'll start lifting out the frames.

Rondo: Allegro vivace

The sky sets out its corners like a composer assembling phrases.
Hidden oranges rot in the nasturtiums.
From here I can picture

the new branch nearly bent,
its summer burst of fruit
and fall; the honeycombs,

their shingled lobes
broken off and bursting wax caps as they drip
the short course to the lips and tongue;

and the bits of wax that will stick to my hands
like the breeze now that lifts
the months-old coolness from the ground

so that the temperatures mix around my waist,
clinging to my fingers
with the dirt and radish burrs,

the wish to be at both
the near end and the unspoiled start,
curled to each other like

the weight of one step to the next—
the best part, and the best part—

the sky sets out its corners,
my neighbors each appear with mud shoes, clippers,
and the oranges rot, gorgeously, in the nasturtiums.

The sauce

Plump red globes just picked, halved and tossed in oil and salt—roast them long and slow. Press through the mill—no skin or seed—just flesh and juice, warm as earth—

Or minced root and stem, sweet in the pan. Add wine, the broth from shells. More and less, like late sun eked thin on the long flank of earth—not quite gone—pink and gold and full of its own salt, and not much else—

Or tear the leaves in strips, with oil and salt, plump seed, gored bulb. Crush so it all bleeds green, like bits of shell left in the tide, like a storm, like its smell, like the slick and foam-pocked skin of the sea—

Just taste. There should not be too much. Fork and bread, tongue and salt. It should fill your dreams and raise the sea. It should be enough.

The room

The sink at a height and of a depth that one's arms could hang like leaves while the hands were at work with the tap and the soap and the brush on the glass and the pan and the dish. And the panes set just so in the wall so that the late light would drape the eyes and neck.

The floor tiles: large squares of deep red and bone white. The cool seams could be felt on the soles of the feet. Crumbs could stick there. It could tilt. It could spill.

The dry cloth. The struck match. Walls steel-blue, gone to white.

The size of the room could change. Air would go through, and up, while light would stay. The guest, the host. Heat from the stove would smell like a storm. Would feel like brushed wool. Would sound like no one heard. Rain could come. Fog. Disgust. I would cook them all up. I would feed them all well.

Beef stew,

cold, in the pot, in the fridge. Take it out and
set it on the stove top, heat on low. Fine blue stripe of flame.
Put my bag down.
Wash up, change my clothes, check the pot,
turn the heat up. Get a beer from the fridge.
Give the pot a stir.
Put a tape on,
sit down. Bare foot up on my knee.
Then: horns,
plucked bass.
And the car horns on the street, the sky's
big blue still warm, far-off,
and then just horns.
Give the pot a stir. And he comes in,
hear his feet on the stairs and he
comes in. Kiss on the neck, kiss on the cheek,
kiss on the lips. He cleans up,
he sips at my beer, he sits down.
I give it a stir. Get two bowls
and spoon it out. Him in his chair,
me in mine. Take
a bite—*oh Lord*
hot hot.
Sip at the beer. And the far-off blue less
warm, less
far-off. That one point
just in reach. Give it a stir. And take
a bite, *oh*

oh hot so
good, so
warm on its way down, just like
that kiss
and still horns, still him
with his bowl there, and the horns,
and the steam, and time less tense, time
turned in and kind of loose,
and I give it a stir, sip
at the beer, so
good, so glad
I made it, so
glad I made it,
yesterday.

Three weeknight dinners involving eggs

The omelette

Standing at the counter, the radio, the news, pick the leaves off the herbs that you cut from the yard coming home. Smell your fingers. Pour the beer into the glass. Break the eggs and beat them, adding salt and herbs and pepper. In the pan, a slab of butter, and working quickly: pour the eggs into the perfect circle that turns pale and firm on the underside and edges, where you gather back the hem and let the liquid part spill over—

shaking it until it folds itself together, and it's ready, soft envelope of happiness, slipped onto the plate and you cut a slice, wet sound of lightness breaking—

like the perfect day you didn't have, split open—

the late light through the window, the radio, your dinner;
the pan is still hot and you have your back to it:
you, and the beer, and the omelette.

The pizza

Because the ragged day requires something round, put your bag on the chair, turn on the oven and the radio, lift the large bowl down from its shelf above the window. Foam the yeast in the water with a little sugar, stir in oil, salt, and flour—then turn it out, and knead, and set the dough aside to rise—

Start the eggs to boil, and peel and chop the garlic and oregano, listen to the eggs rattle gently on the stainless steel. Then lift them with the slotted spoon to the ice and water, squeeze, the flake of shell and cling, and steam—

The dough rolled and turned onto the floured peel, with oil and garlic in the oven till the bubbles harden into crust like brittle stars, and slid

onto the table and spread round with anchovies, sliced egg, the oregano sprinkled over. Now divide it, as you do each morning with your heart. Start again: Begin with any slice, and eat the whole thing up.

The serendipitous cold plate

Yes, the radio. Put the bread from your bag on the counter. There is some leathery golden Gouda. The rest of the eggs you boiled last night. Watercress. The end of a white wine that tastes like wildflowers.

Change your shoes. And thus suddenly inspired, peel the eggs, slice in half and mash the yolks with mayonnaise and mustard, salt and pepper, paprika—

and—*Yes!*—capers—

and as you finish getting little bits of it on all your fingers, listen to the traffic; as you arrange it on the plate, to the sunlight dip below the roofs, to the outer lives of all your neighbors being tucked into their cedar drawers, to a football hit the pavement and complete its long and trembling arc.

Cadence

*for Lou and the Oaktown Café, where you could
have lunch whenever the oven was hot*

Lunch at three.
My stool at the counter.
That pizza and I

are destined for each other. Both slowly
warmed by minutes. This is nearly
the best part: before

I eat. Pamina sings
of Tamino in *The Magic Flute*.
Then the joyous, simple

echoed lines as they emerge
from their ordeals. Before
each other, faces

round and warm. The sun
comes out. The slice
resolves upon the tongue.

Goddess Arias　　*for mezzo-soprano*

Goddess of the Crosswords

Let's go where the grapes are. It's
peaceful there, surrounded by the hush
of office fans. After lunch, a little

congregation round the sink—librarians all
brush their teeth, then return to work.
Bees approach, trailing purpose

like some fabulous perfume.
It's always early afternoon,
and no one else around.

Goddess of the Donuts

Let's forget ourselves in music, notes
ascending in an order you
remember, like

you remember, each morning, waking in bed,
that this is good. Choice
and completeness

snore lightly at your ankles, un-
distinguishable from the blankets.

Goddess of the Hazards

Let's consider. Goodness
clings to the surface, gold leaf
on its square of tissue. The train

screams overhead. Love rests
in its small boat of silence, one eye open.

Goddess of the Bass

Let's understand something from the start:
The world is kind of an arbitrary mess.
Morning already sold

out—a special revue with added numbers.
Meanwhile, in the highway-bordered orchards,
the apples sweeten. They

hang on. They under-
study the chorus. They are prepared
to stop at the top of their form.

Goddess of the Dial Tone

Let's not be too hasty.
This storm may be days in coming.
Most projects,

like this, are never ending.
The marmalade
is hesitating on the stove,

the roots of transplants
unwind bravely in the dirt.

Goddess of the Sugar Cubes

Let's pretend we're at the castle.
Cribbage, and the music of woodwinds.
Everyone sipping

limoncello, and the resident
ghosts reading the paper.
Occasional "pfft"s

from their insubstantial lips
ripple the pages; their long toes
shiver.

Goddess of Sanity and Dismay

Let's not forget the longest night.
The ruminating beasts that feed on dreams.
The corncakes and pretzels,

the ice cream, salami,
and string cheese. The chilly distance.
The rubber-banding distress.

The weather-beaten occupants,
placing roses
on all the threadbare hours.

TODAY'S SPECIAL DISH

Today's special dish

It was the morning's sweetness, a cold wind
on warm air and the papery smell

of wisteria, that tempted me to homemade tortellini
for your lunch. Now, broth

simmering, the pasta is dry
and cracking in my fingers. The last time we spoke

was like this,
frazzled, rushed, marked by a kiss for the sake

of notifying you that I still love you.
Now I want to start over.

Plain noodles in butter.
Kissing by the kitchen window.

I love you perfectly when you are gone—please picture
how I intend to treat you. As if just the thought

should make it true: the tortellini
in the pot—broth blossoming—the dumplings suddenly plump, and soft.

The 40 comes after the 12

You rolled in so late last night after the lecture
"about the inherent dissatisfaction in
the impermanence of everything" that my dreams

were full of your returning; over
and over you came to me, long into
the early morning—

and I know what you mean, I
guess, here at the bus stop admiring
the verisimilitude of permanence:

the sun rises, the doors
at Walgreens open automatically
as if someone were there,
the 40 comes after the 12,

I miss you when I leave, and it seems
it has been this way for longer
than I can remember—a ribbon

that will keep unwinding, not
forever, but for as long as it matters.

The night we missed the aurora borealis,

rarely seen this far south and red with high-
altitude oxygen,

we were eating soba and declining
quickly towards sleep,

which had been eluding us
as first one rolled

toward it, then the other, un-
synchronous symphony

of sheets and covers—
but which that night,

fed properly and reduced
into the requisite arrangement of energy, burst

and formed a coupled dream
of so awesome a color

it buzzed around and through us like the perfect dinner,
like charged particles blown in from the sun—

Listen

I was telling you something and at some point

stopped listening. The frogs were croaking in the neighbor's yard, the Children's
Hospital helicopter descending.

Evening. I thought of the musicians, the endless lengths
of rehearsals. *This way, this way*. The poets. The sadly muddled

people who sit down, uninvited, at your table.
Thirteen variations of meat sauce with rigatoni. I was telling you something

and at some point stopped listening. It was evening. I was all un-
done, had lost my stitching. You sat there holding one frayed end,

converting weariness to patience, and I could hear you doing it,
as if an entire audience depended on this—

Neglect

nothing. The breath mint
admired for its power of transition.

The large crumb
of fallen ricotta pie that I stepped on last night,

removed. Your side
of the bed

turned down
so that you'll remember to come home, so that

I can sleep. But paying such
close attention, I fear the streets

will buckle behind my back, the city
slither closer to the water,

nasturtiums send out their blatant runners—
and I'll have done it again: chosen

the wrong kind of beauty, or chosen beauty
over happiness.

How it feels

Finally, the ants seem to understand.
After days of painstakingly disrupting their paths
through the bathroom, first to the shower, then

to the discarded lid of a pint of ice cream in the wastebasket,
and finally to the minute pool of water caught

in the plastic wrapper on the twenty-four pack of toilet paper—
after days of suggesting

in my own barbaric way (Windex) that they find another venue,
they decide to leave.
I come home

unbelt, drop my nice trousers and sit down to see
that finally they are all traveling back up their trail, to the window
(pausing to assist those carrying the wounded),

except for an adventurous couple of dozen
caught now, in the middle of the room,

scurrying round the damp bath mat—
they've lost the trail,
they touch heads

and say to each other: Who are you?
Where are we?
Where does a body go from here?

The trouble with progress

There is an expectation.
It waits behind things, carefully. When it moves
it kicks up a great wind with its shoulders,
toppling crockery.

It would like to be
the thing expected: its arrival. A favorite
hour. The encore. The squid-ink risotto, put before you. Or even the un-
expected thing,

the earwig in the jar of beans.
Lightning in December. It would be willing
to travel backwards, to be

the moment before
you expected anything—that small,
yellow moment. It was square, like a postage stamp,
and so patient.

Plot twist

Things are changing.
Yesterday I did not send back
my hamburger, overcooked. Christmas

sales are strangling themselves. The wind
is rising, a few persimmons cling.
Morning squeezes

through, pink. The world
had been shrinking; now it's gotten
suddenly wider, like a dangerous river.

Last night a movie
left us speechless. We four walked back to the car
like bees repeating a dance. I held your hand

in the back seat, and through the night in bed.
The dreams were like a boat,
the sleep a country,

the night an author
that found us to be somewhat unsatisfactory characters.
Please let me remember.

Repair

Haggard doves and delivery vans
prowl around morning's scene
of general disaster. Rain showers

won't stop flooding the gutters.
At the café we don't
really pay attention,

we are reading the "East Bay Living" section,
the comics, the reviews, the April travel
ads. Every now and then

one person looks up,
and down. We all think
we are in the same lifeboat. And we don't

delude ourselves lightly—
we go about it with the same care you take
with newborns, with pastries,

with the Christmas present you unwrapped
once, in the middle of the night, underneath the tree,
knowing too much to sleep,

a longer distance ahead,
love oddly steadier for the disappointment,
and hope only slightly blemished.

Problem

There are the things in my head
and the things before me.
They rub against each other, like two ships about to destroy each other.
There are the lists I left on the table.
Pine needles dropping from the wreath to the windowsill.
The parents outside my window, rushing to drop off their children and
      driving far too fast and swerving dangerously.
The backpacks made in China that flap against the children's backs like
      children jumping double Dutch.
There are the children who cannot double Dutch.
There are the billions of small, weedy fears blooming in those children's heads,
and the tall, glorious fears that have taken over my body, startling and brilliant.
There are the ants under my house.
The ants under your house.
The figs that the ants are after.
There are the chocolate truffles, and the almond wafers.
The jars of olives, capers, pickles, that gasp and pop.
The crates of rations traveling the world and not getting there in time.
Nineteen varieties of snack-sized fruit yogurts sitting on refrigerated shelves.
Thickets of discarded fries after the lunch rush at McDonald's.
There are the limbs of the buried and unburied after the tsunami.
The disasters at work about which I try to casually laugh.
The days of chilling rain in which melancholy and happiness trade places,
and the moments of blue sky between storms.
There are the hours I've slept in his arms.
There are the many days I don't know how my body manages to hold itself
      together, but it does.

There are the things in my head I will not tell you about, for reasons I will not
    tell you about.
There are the things before me that I will not tell you about, for similar reasons.
There are things that are mine, just mine,
just as you have yours,
in this world where we have nothing we don't pay for, dearly,
in this world of things that inhabit us, that make us grind our teeth unconsciously
    all night,
beautiful, terrible things that I cannot live without.

Infrangible

It was a mess of a poem I was reading, about the universe
and eating. Chickens figured in it,

desire, snails,
and the patterns of kitchen tiles. It had
that unlikely word in it

which turned out to really be a word,
but who needs a poem you have to look up to believe?
I was looking for the poem that would make everything better

and it seemed productive
to start with the assumption that I
was insignificant,

that all my striving for culture was laughable,
and that I was a fool surrounded by idiots.
Civilization thus

reduced to the mediocre,
suddenly everything did seem better.
I arrived at coffee,

and everyone I'd ever known was there,
and the clouds set up
their half-hearted stations, and the dogs

sniffed each other's butts,
the hills slowly undressed themselves,
the soundtrack

swelled with Brazilian guitars—
and the paper moon set with hopes of a reprise,
and the coffee was warm and only a little off.

Under it all

There is nothing above it all,
nothing—anyway—to breathe.

Down here: relief, crushed
street plums underfoot, the smell of bacon,
sprinklers misfiring,
the sound of too many women

trying to decide something, and a bus
hurrying, and all of the espresso machines in a quarter-mile radius hissing—

Plasticky light glaring from car hoods,
the stuffy shade of awnings,
the yawning interiors of beauty parlors
and the smoky smell of singed hair—

Above, apparently, there is splendor, peace, no need to justify
the humble ambitions of dandelions,

but under it all, after all, I have hot dogs
and ice cream, precious coffee, mild assurance,
the pleasant hum of general malaise,
Cheerios that clutch the surface of the milk,

the stub ends of pleasure, Cabernet and peanut brittle,
the pot of water shivering on the stove,
the familiar limits of human ability to rise to the occasion,
and all my friends, assembled here for nothing.

That'll be one dollar

Morning, again, what luck.
The gray sky is smooth and glassy. I feel sure

this is the morning
they'll give me a free cup of coffee.

Everyone here is regular. They'll all share the paper;
it's practice for the motions of the day,

when we each relinquish ownership
of making ourselves happy. There is a trick

to coming home whole again, but I couldn't
tell you how, exactly; it tends to leave me

like a dream.
Mornings always make me a little nervous, this way, then

a little thankful, like sitting down to watch a mystery
that's still a mystery, even though it's one I know I've seen.

Recapitulation

And once, I thought this wasn't enough.
The train is in the tunnel, then
enters my old beloved life—sun
flickers in the cut-crystal graffiti-scratched window.
The car is full but quiet. No one has completely
shaken off the thoughtfulness of sleep.
The city spreads its belly. A schoolgirl
with her mother sucks her finger. Yes,
I remember this. Residue of fog surrounds us all in brilliance.
And the betrayal was my own, not the world's
but mine, because I'd gotten in my own way,
because I'd doubted this was love.

NOTES

"Hero Portraits": These portraits were inspired by artworks and written comments of other artists exhibited at the Oakland Museum of California and the San Francisco Museum of Modern Art.

Untitled (verso of *Untitled*), *Approximate Man*, *Sublime Aspect*, *Cheerful Aspect*, *Man with a Wing*, and *The Saint of Inner Light*, are all titles of works by Paul Klee.

Untitled (formerly *Self-Portrait*) is a painting by Clyfford Still.

Self-Portrait in a Toaster is a photograph by Rondal Partridge. "I said 'Hold it,'" "He wanted to arrest me, and I said I refused to be arrested," "They had to dance with each other—there were no women around," "Let me show you my family of cameras," "I love bargains," and "People love radios" are all his words about his own photographs, printed in the "Notes on Plates" section of his exhibition catalog, *Quizzical Eye: The Photography of Rondal Partridge*, by Elizabeth Partridge and Sally Stein, published by the California Historical Society Press, © 2003. "Dark and Light" is the title of the afterword by Elizabeth Partridge in that catalog.

"Overture": An Italian overture usually has three movements: the first and last ones generally faster, in the major key, and the middle one slower, often in the minor key. The first movement was the precursor to the sonata form. The last movement is often a dance form.

"The room": Inspired by Elizabeth David's description of her ideal kitchen in *The Art of Kitchen Design* by Johnny Grey (Cassell, 2002).

"Cadence": In music, a cadence (from Latin *cadentia*, "falling") is a melodic arrangement of intervals that indicates the end of an idea, creating a sense of rest.

"Recapitulation": In music, the recapitulation is the third and last section of the sonata form, restating the theme and offering a resolution for the harmonic conflicts.

Also from Sixteen Rivers Press

In Search of Landscape, by Helen Wickes
The Long Night of Flying, by Sharon Olson
Any Old Wolf, by Murray Silverstein
In the Right Season, by Diane Sher Lutovich
Mapmaker of Absences, by Maria M. Benet
Swimmer Climbing onto Shore, by Gerald Fleming
No Easy Light, by Susan Sibbet
Falling World, by Lynn Lyman Trombetta
Sacred Precinct, by Jacqueline Kudler
What I Stole, by Diane Sher Lutovich
After Cocteau, by Carolyn Miller
Snake at the Wrist, by Margaret Kaufman
Translations from the Human Language, by Terry Ehret
difficult news, by Valerie Berry

SIXTEEN RIVERS PRESS is a shared-work, nonprofit poetry collective dedicated to providing an alternate publishing avenue for San Francisco Bay Area poets. Founded in 1999 by seven writers, the press is named for the sixteen rivers that flow into the San Francisco Bay.

SAN JOAQUIN · FRESNO · CHOWCHILLA · MERCED · TUOLOMNE · STANISLAUS · CALAVERAS · BEAR · MOKELUMNE · COSUMNES · AMERICAN · YUBA · FEATHER · SACRAMENTO · NAPA · PETALUMA